Mark Pett

Cottonwood Press, Inc.
Fort Collins, Colorado

Copyright © 2002 by Mark Pett

All rights reserved. No part of this book may be reproduced
or utilized in any form or by any means,
electronic or mechanical, including photocopying, recording
or any information storage or retrieval system,
without the written permission of the publisher.

Requests for permission should be addressed to:

Cottonwood Press, Inc.
107 Cameron Drive
Fort Collins, CO 80525
800-864-4297
www.cottonwoodpress.com

ISBN 1-877673-55-2

About Mr. Lowe...

CAL LOWE. New 4th grade teacher.

Extracurricular Activities: Hanging out with friend Abigail; getting dragged on extreme sports outings with roommate Gus.

Best Known For: His lack of control in the classroom; his idealism; a determination to never give up on his students.

In 1994, cartoonist Mark Pett put his artistic career on hold to work in Mississippi's public schools. Teaching sixth grade confirmed Pett's beliefs that (1) a good education is imperative for America's children, and (2) 12-year-olds are spawns of the devil.

It's not that he didn't love the children he worked with. They were smart and funny, and could melt your heart with a smile. He just realized that novice, idealistic teachers are to 12-year-olds what friendly little bunnies are to wolves. After two years in the classroom, Mark had a newfound respect for teachers — he now ranks them right up there with world peace negotiators and people who repair VCRs.

"Mr. Lowe" is a comic strip loosely based on Mark's own experiences as a teacher. Formerly syndicated as a newspaper comic strip, "Mr. Lowe" is a tribute to all the unsung heroes who manage our nation's classrooms. It is also a tribute to the kids who aggravate those unsung heroes.

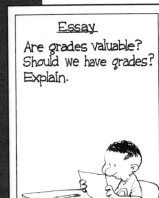

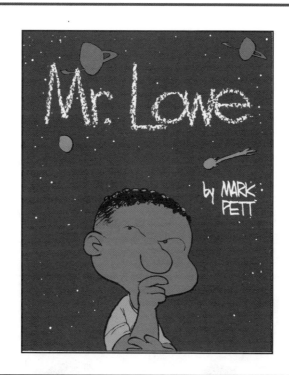

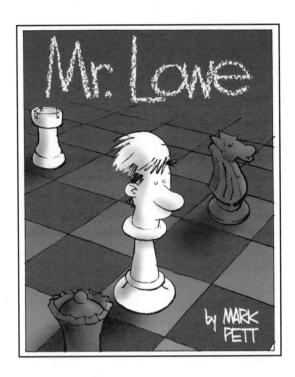

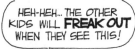

About the Author...

Mark Pett grew up in Utah. After graduating from the University of Pennsylvania, where he turned in a cartoon of his professor for his linear algebra final, he left the country to work as an editorial cartoonist in Prague. He soon learned that Czechs don't have the same appreciation Americans do for having their political leaders depicted without pants.

Back in the states, Pett's work appeared in all the major Utah publications, including The Salt Lake Tribune, Deseret News, Salt Lake City Weekly, and The Enterprise. The Society of Professional Journalists named him Utah's most outstanding editorial cartoonist in 1998.

Mark Pett currently resides in Cambridge, Massachusetts, with his wife Tiffany and their two dogs.

TO ORDER MORE COPIES OF MR. LOWE...

Please send me _____ copies of Mr. Lowe. I am enclosing $12.95, plus shipping and handling ($4.00 for one book, $2.00 for each additional book). Colorado residents add 39¢ sales tax per book. Total amount $_____.

Name _____

(School) _____
(Include only if using school address.)

Phone _____

Address _____

City _____ State _____ Zip Code _____

Method of Payment:

❏ Payment enclosed ❏ Credit Card ❏ Purchase Order (must include)

Credit Card# _____ Expiration Date _____

Signature _____

Send to:

COTTONWOOD PRESS INC.
107 Cameron Drive
Fort Collins, CO 80525
1-800-864-4297
www.cottonwoodpress.com